RADICAL HOSPITALITY

LEADER'S GUIDE

FOR 13 GROUP-STUDY SESSIONS

Dorothy J. Pellegri
David and Ruth Rupprecht

Presbyterian and Reformed Publishing Company
Phillipsburg, New Jersey

Used by permission. This leader's guide was developed for Presbyterian and Reformed Publishing Company by Arbuta House.

ISBN 0-87552-419-2

PREFACE

Purpose of This Study: The aim of this study is to build up God's people and promote the conversion of the lost. The ministry of radical hospitality provides a number of very practical and specific ways in which that twofold purpose can be achieved.

Scope of This Study: The book *Radical Hospitality* was designed to be read by those contemplating the ministry of a healing household, or those who see the need for such an outreach even though they themselves are unable to minister in this way. But it is also designed to be studied in church groups—by boards of elders seeking direction for church ministries, or church school classes—any group of Christians who believe each church should be reaching out in this way. This study considers the concept of radical hospitality through reading David and Ruth Rupprecht's book, integrating it with key passages of Scripture, and seeking to apply it through creating the structure that best suits a particular church's setting and experiences. Other sources such as additional readings and interviews with local ministering families are also an inspirational, practical, and integral part of this study.

Specific Goals of This Study

1. To understand the meaning of radical hospitality as it is taught in the Scriptures.
2. To discover specific methods for participating in radical hospitality.
3. To become aware of dangerous pitfalls for one participating in radical hospitality.

Recommended General Preparation for the Leader

1. Read through the textbook giving specific attention to Scripture references, key concepts, and specific lists.

2. Skim the leader's guide to see what lies ahead. Pay attention to recommended leader preparations in each session and any special equipment needed so that you do not get caught off guard at the last moment. Also look at special assignments given to students. You will always want to be prepared to make up for any failures on the part of students to do their assignments.

3. Look at the bibliography and seek access to as many of its resources as possible.

4. Several sections of this study require an overhead projector or chalkboard. We recommend the use of an overhead for large classes and when it is possible to prepare transparencies before class. On other occasions a white marker board is far superior to the traditional chalkboard.

Session Plan: Each session is provided with a plan that follows the following format:

Teaching Objectives: These will begin with the words, "The student will be able to . . . ." If it is not clear to you what the responses should be, these can usually be found in the answers to the review or discussion questions.

Recommended Student Preparation

Recommended Teacher Preparation: When something additional to the student preparation is recommended.

Recommended Use of Class Time: This assumes a 50-minute period. You have to adjust for a longer or shorter period. Also remember that this is *recommended* use. You may want to do other things. Also do not be upset if you do not cover all the material. We have tried to give you more than enough.

Review Questions: Answers to these should be easily obtained with a Scripture reference or a reference to the textbook.

Discussion Questions: These may have long and complicated answers or more than one right answer.

Note: Sometimes the review and discussion questions will be incorporated into the recommended use of class time. Also, you may wish to supplement the review and discussion questions with questions of your own. We have given questions here that are thought provoking or fundamental to the teaching objectives. We have not listed the obvious questions that can be asked of almost every passage: What is the Scripture talking about here? How would you put this in your own words? etc.

Leader's Self-Evaluation: It is recommended that the leader continuously do a self-evaluation. At the end of each session, ask the following questions and keep a written record of the answers.

1. Did the entire session work toward the accomplishment of the goals stated for this course? If there were digressions, how did they occur and how can such be avoided in the future?
2. Were the students able to meet the teaching objectives? If not, why not?
3. Was anything not made clear in this session that should be clarified in the next?
4. Are there individuals with whom I should have a personal conversation to clarify something, to encourage, etc.?

Course Overview

Session and Topic	*Textbook Readings*	*Scripture Readings*
1. Introduction		Romans 12:9–16
2. Radical Hospitality	Chapters 1, 2	Luke 14:1–35
3. The Biblical Basis	Chapter 3	Isaiah 58:5–12; James 2:15–17; I John 3:17, 18; Deuteronomy 10:19; I Chronicles 29:10–19
4. Meeting the Needs	Chapters 4, 5	Matthew 25:34–46
5. Self-Evaluation	Pages 43–53 Activities 1, 2 on pages 60, 61	I Peter 3:8–10
6. God's Calling and Leading	Pages 53–61	Luke 14:28–30
7. The Recipient	Chapter 7	I Corinthians 2:12–16
8. Dealing with Parents	Chapter 8 Activity 2 on page 84	Ephesians 6:1–4; II Corinthians 5:17–21
9. Setting Goals and Bounds, I	Chapter 9	Philippians 3:13b, 14; Colossians 3:8–17
10. Setting Goals and Bounds, II	Chapter 9 Activities on pages 101	I Corinthians 3:6–11
11. The Local Church	Chapter 10 Activities 1, 2 on page 108	Ephesians 4:11–16; I Corinthians 12:18–20
12. Prayer	Chapter 11	Philippians 1:9–11
13. Building the Local Model		I Corinthians 1:4–9

Class Deletion Contingency: If it becomes necessary to cancel a class during the course, the following is recommended: combine classes 1 and 2, 9 and 10, or 12 and 13.

SESSION 1

Introduction

Romans 12:9–16

Teaching Objective: The student will be able to state the purpose, scope, and goals of this course in his or her own words.

Recommended Student Preparation: No preparation is necessary for this first session.

Recommended Leader Preparation

1. See the first page of this leader's guide, "General Preparation for the Leader."

2. Have paper and pencils available for any members of the class who may not have them.

Recommended Use of Class Time: This assumes a 50-minute period.

1. Begin with prayer. (2 min.)

2. Ask the students to write a definition of hospitality, using Scripture to support their definition. (3 min. Let this overlap the next item of business.)

3. Attend to administrative matters. Distribute books, take attendance, etc. as required by your school. You may reproduce the course overview, questions for review and discussion, and bibliography for distribution to the class. (5 min.)

4. Discuss the purpose, scope, and specific goals of this course as they are stated in the front of this guide. (6 min.)

5. Collect and read some of the students' definitions of hospi-

tality. Use your own discretion as to how many definitions to read, but be sure to include as many varying definitions as possible. Read the textbook, page 13, paragraph 1. (9 min.)

6. Assign various class members to read aloud some of the following passages. (Time may prevent you from using all of them.) Discuss and list the various ways hospitality is shown and to whom it may be directed. Be sure to mention the goals and purposes for these ministries. Sum up by using the review and discussion questions. (18 min.)

   a. Luke 10:30–37; Proverbs 3:27, 28
   b. II Kings 4:8–10
   c. Matthew 25:34–40
   d. Matthew 9:10–12
   e. Romans 12:9–16; I Peter 4:8–10
   f. Titus 1:7, 8
   g. Psalms 68:6
   h. Isaiah 58:5–9
   i. James 2:15–17

7. Go over review and discussion questions. (5 min.)

8. Give the assignment for the next session. See recommended student preparation under the next session. (1 min.)

9. Close in prayer. (1 min.)

Review Questions

1. What is the purpose of this course? (See the first page of the leader's guide.)

2. What are the goals of this course? (See the first page of the leader's guide.)

3. What different forms does hospitality take? (See the texts listed under "Recommended Use of Class Time," number 6.)

Discussion Questions: These do not necessarily have one right answer.

1. How would you change your definition of hospitality in light of the class discussions so far?

2. So far we have spoken of "hospitality." How do you anticipate that the authors will modify the meaning of hospitality by

calling it "radical hospitality"?

3. What forms of hospitality have you been practicing and how do they match your talents?

4. What fears might you have concerning practicing hospitality? What Scripture can you think of that would dispel these fears? Try to distinguish between excuses and fears.

5. What is the difference between entertaining and hospitality? How could an over-emphasis on the former interfere with true hospitality?

Alternate or Additional Activities

1. Use the five discussion questions in the next session as a questionnaire. Substitute "Christian" for "radical" since "radical" hospitality may throw the students off track. Use this as a pretest to see where the class now stands on hospitality or use this instead of asking them to define hospitality.

2. Ask the students to answer in writing: What do you hope to learn from this course? This could be very beneficial to you!

SESSION 2

Radical Hospitality

Luke 14:1–35

Teaching Objectives

1. The student will be able to explain how the authors define *radical* hospitality. (See the second sentence of the first paragraph on page 14 of the textbook.)

2. The student will be able to list the three components of such a ministry. (See the numbered paragraphs on pages 14, 15.)

Recommended Student Preparation

1. Read the textbook, chapters 1 and 2.
2. Look for a definition of radical hospitality.
3. Interview one family that has regularly shown a form of hospitality discussed in session 1. Make a list of both the problems and the blessings they experienced. This list is to be shared with the class. (Leader: If you really think this will flop, see the alternate activity at the end of this session.)

Recommended Leader Preparation: Scan chapter titles in some of the books listed in the bibliography for material that may help you in this session. Particularly note Mains, 1975 and Jackson, 1974.

Recommended Use of Class Time: This assumes a 50-minute period.

1. Scripture reading: Luke 14:1–35. (2 min.)
2. Prayer. (2 min.)

3. Administrative matters. Attendance, etc. as required by your school. (2 min.)

4. Review the last session by using its review questions and perhaps one or two discussion questions if you did not get to them last week. (5 min.)

5. Discuss the definition of radical hospitality (textbook, page 14, paragraph 1, second sentence) and have the students discuss the two meanings of "radical": basic and extreme. Use the following questions for discussion (these may not have only one right answer): Is there a need for radical hospitality? Is there a biblical command for radical hospitality? Explain that in the next two sessions the class will try to answer these questions. (10 min.)

6. Have the students share their homework interviews with the class. (Or see the alternate activity.) (10 min.)

7. List the three components of radical hospitality, preferably on an overhead transparency, and briefly discuss them and how the examples from chapter 1 and the interviews compare. Tie together the points the author is making—that is the three numbered paragraphs on pages 14–16. (17 min.)

8. Use review and discussion questions as time permits.

9. Give the assignment for next session. See recommended student preparation under the next session. (1 min.)

10. Close in prayer. (1 min.)

Review Questions

1. What is radical hospitality? (See the textbook, page 14, paragraph 1.)

2. What are the three components of such a ministry? (See the numbered paragraphs on pages 14, 15 of the textbook.)

Discussion Questions: These do not necessarily have one right answer.

1. How would you define radical hospitality?

2. Have you ever been on the giving end of radical hospitality? Please explain.

3. Have you ever been on the receiving end of radical hospitality? Please explain.

4. Have you ever been in need of radical hospitality and not received it? Please explain.

5. How could you be supportive of others in the church who are extending radical hospitality?

Additional or Alternate Learning Activity

Break into small groups to discuss Luke 14:12–14 and to explore the new meaning Jesus gives to hospitality. Ask the students to identify the following:

a. Jesus' audience
b. The heart attitude Jesus perceived
c. The principles of hospitality we find here

After small-group discussions, ask these questions of the reassembled class to sum up the discussion.

SESSION **3**

The Biblical Basis

Isaiah 58:5–12

Teaching Objectives

1. The student will be able to explain who the alien and stranger is in the Old and New Testament teachings.
2. The student will be able to cite at least one Scripture passage that gives a command regarding the alien.

Recommended Student Preparation

1. Read the textbook, chapter 3.
2. Read Isaiah 58:1–12; James 2:15–17; I John 3:17, 18; Deuteronomy 10:19; and I Chronicles 29:10–19.

Recommended Leader Preparation

1. Scan the books listed in the bibliography for material helpful to you in this session. Note particularly Foster, 1981 and De Vaux, 1965.
2. If possible, obtain "Isaiah 58" on the Sparrow Records recording by John Michael Talbot and Terry Talbot. Play this instead of having a Scripture reading.

Recommended Use of Class Time: This assumes a 50-minute period.

1. Scripture reading: Isaiah 58:5–12. (2 min.)
2. Prayer. (2 min.)
3. Administrative matters. Attendance, etc. as required by your school. (2 min.)

4. Review by using some of the review questions from previous sessions. (5 min.)

5. Divide the class into two groups. (If it is a particularly large class, divide it into four groups, two of which will deal with one topic and two with the other.) The groups will consider the concept of alien and stranger as it is found in the Old and New Testaments respectively. The Old Testament group should consider Deuteronomy 10:19; I Chronicles 29:10–19; Exodus 22:21; 23:9; and Leviticus 19:9, 10. The New Testament group should consider Ephesians 2:11–22 and I Peter 2:9–12. Each group should try to identify how the alien was treated and why he was treated that way. (15 min.)

6. Receive reports from the groups. (7 min.)

7. Try as a class to relate the Old and New Testament concepts in your minds. Look at Isaiah 58:6–12; James 2:15–17; and I John 3:17, 18 together as a class. (15 min.)

8. Use review and discussion questions as time permits.

9. Give the assignment for next session. See recommended student preparation under the next session. (1 min.)

10. Close in prayer. (1 min.)

Review Questions

1. What is one Old Testament reference that gives a command regarding the alien or stranger?

2. What is one New Testament reference that gives a command regarding the alien or stranger?

3. What are three principles that the authors of our textbook stress in chapter 3? (1. Each of us can identify with the alien and stranger for we too have been aliens and strangers. 2. We are to imitate God, who is our ultimate host. 3. We are called to minister to the needs of the whole man.)

Discussion Questions: These do not necessarily have one right answer.

1. Compare the differences between American views of hospitality and those of other countries. How have independence, privacy, and isolation interfered with the practice of hospitality?

2. Do the New Testament passages read refer only to showing hospitality towards other Christians? If so, is this the teaching throughout the New Testament?

Additional or Alternate Learning Activity: Discuss with the class the concept that God is our heavenly perfect example (or host, although this is not what "God of Hosts" means) in His dealings with the alien and stranger. Use Scriptures such as I Chronicles 29:15; Isaiah 25:6; Psalm 23:6; Luke 15:11–32; and Revelation 19:7–10.

SESSION **4**

Meeting the Needs

Matthew 25:34–46

Teaching Objectives

1. The student will be able to list some of the social needs that radical hospitality can meet in a variety of settings.

2. The student will be able to define the end product of radical hospitality as an independent yet God dependent person.

Recommended Student Preparation

1. Read the textbook, chapters 4 and 5.

2. Read Matthew 25:34–46.

3. During the week, check the newspaper or television news for stories of those in need of radical hospitality and note the method of presentation and the slant of the announcer or writer.

4. If you desire to use the alternate or additional activity, ask one student to give a book report on John Perkins's, *A Quiet Revolution*, 1977. The student would not necessarily have to read the entire book. You may want to make it easier for him by locating the book and bringing it to class.

Recommended Leader Preparation: You may want to do some reading in Perkins, 1977 and be prepared in case the student does not succeed in getting his homework done.

Recommended Use of Class Time: This assumes a 50-minute period.

1. Scripture reading: Matthew 25:34–46. (2 min.)

2. Prayer. (2 min.)

3. Administrative matters. Attendance, etc. as required by your school. (2 min.)

4. Ask the students to report on what they have observed in the news media about those in need of radical hospitality. Then review the three biblical principles that are the basis of radical hospitality as they were discussed in chapter 3 of the textbook. (1. Each of us can identify with the alien and stranger for we too have been aliens and strangers. 2. We are to imitate God who is our ultimate host. 3. We are called to minister to the needs of the whole man.) (10 min.)

5. Review what the authors of our textbook had to say in chapter 4. React to their statement that the goal of radical hospitality is "an independent and yet God dependent person living in, but not of the world" (page 27, last paragraph). Is this an adequate statement of the goal? Is it a biblical goal? (7 min.)

6. On an overhead projector or marker board write the categories the authors use for recipients of radical hospitality: "Dependent," "Superindependent," and "Withdrawn" (pages 27, 28). Have the class comment on the suggestions made for meeting the needs of each. How is radical hospitality useful? What problem does each type bring? How valid are the comments on stress? (10 min.)

7. Using chapter 5, discuss the four ministering families that are highlighted. What similarities are found? How do they differ and why? What aspects of God's leading do you see? How do their gifts fit their ministries? (15 min.)

8. Use review and discussion questions as time permits.

9. Give the assignment for next session. See recommended student preparation under the next session. (1 min.)

10. Close in prayer. (1 min.)

Review Questions

1. What is radical hospitality? (Opening a Christian home to someone going through a life crisis for the purpose of ministering healing and life.)

2. What are the three components of radical hospitality?

(Mature, stable, Christian families; a local church body; recipient or modern alien and stranger.)

3. What is the biblical basis for radical hospitality? (Being able to identify with the alien and stranger because we too were the same; imitating God, our heavenly example; ministering to the needs of the whole man.)

4. What is the goal or end product of radical hospitality? (An independent yet God dependent person.)

Discussion Questions: These do not necessarily have one right answer.

1. How have social agencies allowed the church to withdraw from its responsibilities? What purpose do social agencies have? Do they have a legitimate purpose?

2. Compare the effectiveness of help through social agencies to the help given through a Christian home and a God-centered value system.

3. Discuss under what circumstances the Christian should make use of social agencies for himself or his guest.

Additional or Alternate Learning Activity: Have a student give a book report on Perkins's book. Discuss it briefly and discuss the need for Christian awareness of social needs. Discuss the possibility of an over-reaction against a "social gospel," producing a "heartless gospel."

SESSION **5**

Self-Evaluation

I Peter 3:8–12

Teaching Objectives

1. The student will be able to evaluate his ability and willingness to deal with the realities of radical hospitality.

2. The student will be able to name the four realities that the authors say must be faced in exercising radical hospitality. (See the boldface subheadings in chapter 6.)

Recommended Student Preparation

1. Read the textbook, pages 43–53.
2. Do activities 1 and 2 of pages 60, 61.
3. Read I Peter 3:8–10.
4. If you choose to do the alternate or additional activity, ask one student to prepare a summary of unit 4 from Wayne Mack's, *Strengthening Your Marriage* (formerly *How to Develop Deep Unity in the Marriage Relationship*).

Recommended Leader Preparation

1. Prepare a book summary as a backup to the one a student may be doing.

2. You may wish to do some reading in Adams's *Christian Living in the Home*, Mack, 1977, or Mains, 1979.

Recommended Use of Class Time: This assumes a 50-minute period.

1. Scripture reading: I Peter 3:8–12. (2 min.)

2. Prayer. (2 min.)

3. Administrative matters. Attendance, etc. as required by your school. (2 min.)

4. Review the last session by using some of its review questions. (5 min.)

5. Discuss the four realities listed in chapter 6. List each reality on the overhead or marker board and ask the students to work through why each is important. Refer to the Scripture reading for this session. If there are some present that have ministered in this way, have them add their own experiences. (10 min.)

6. Read I Corinthians 12:12–28 (or have students read it). Break the group into (a) a married couples' group to discuss their homework activity and this passage—have them also discuss what gifts they might have and what hospitality ministries they might best fill; (b) a singles' group to share what types of gifts they have and the types of hospitality they can offer in view of their singleness. Would any of them consider joining with a couple to form a ministering household? (15 min.)

7. Regroup and share findings with the class. Have the class contribute any suggestions and observed talents the couple may not have considered. Point out that even if class members do not take part in ministering families in radical hospitality, this exercise has great merit and benefit for improving communication. (12 min.)

8. Use review and discussion questions as time permits.

9. Give the assignment for next session. See recommended student preparation under the next session. (1 min.)

10. Close in prayer. (1 min.)

Review Question: What are the four realities of radical hospitality listed in this chapter? (See the boldface subheadings in chapter 6.)

Discussion Questions: These do not necessarily have one right answer.

1. How can the ministry of radical hospitality improve a good or devastate a poor marriage? How might the Lord use this

to sanctify marriages?

2. Discuss the clues that might suggest a poor influence of the guest on the host's children. Have the class give suggestions on how they have dealt with poor influences in the school or the neighborhood on their children in the past.

3. Ask yourselves, Can we realistically qualify as a willing and disciplined household, good for this ministry? If not, are the problems serious enough to warrant corrective action even if you do not open your home for radical hospitality?

Thought Question: Inasmuch as we are to be models of Christian living, how would we evaluate ourselves as examples before our children and neighbors?

Additional or Alternate Learning Activity: Ask one student to prepare and give a summary of unit 4 from Wayne Mack's, *Strengthening Your Marriage* (formerly, *How to Develop Deep Unity in the Marriage Relationship).*

SESSION 6

God's Calling and Leading

Luke 14:28–30

Teaching Objectives

1. The student will be able to evaluate his abilities and willingness to deal with God's calling and leading.

2. The student will be able to list the five steps the authors of the textbook give for trying to discern God's leading.

Recommended Student Preparation

1. Read the textbook, pages 53–61.

2. Read Luke 14:28–30.

3. See "Alternate or Additional Activities" if you intend to use them.

Recommended Leader Preparation

1. Read Schaeffer, 1975, pages 211–234. Read related quotes to the class referring to ways the Schaeffer's were sensitive to family privacy in the midst of many guests who shared their home.

2. Ask a family (outside the class and maybe even the church) to report to the class what factors led them to start a ministry of radical hospitality. If possible, get a couple that have a ministry to foster children or of adoption. Have them talk about problems, adjustments, and blessings. In the next few sessions have other reports from other areas of radical hospitality such as rebellious children, unemployed adults, etc. Let the family know what you have been doing in your class and per-

haps even supply them with a copy of *Radical Hospitality* so that they can interact with it. Allow the class to question them on such things as the legalities, types of agencies, types of need, etc.

Recommended Use of Class Time: This assumes a 50-minute period.

1. Scripture reading: Luke 14:28–30. (2 min.)
2. Prayer. (2 min.)
3. Administrative matters. Attendance, etc. as required by your school. (2 min.)
4. Ask the guest speakers to talk, and glean as much information from them as possible. Encourage the class to ask questions. (talk—15 min.; questions—10 min.)
5. Discuss the section "God's Calling and Leading." Review the steps presented by the authors and ask for brief comments on each. Try to apply them to the visitor's discussion. (12 min.)
6. Read and discuss the prepared quotes from Edith Schaeffer. (5 min.)
7. Use review and discussion questions as time permits.
8. Give the assignment for next session. See recommended student preparation under the next session. (1 min.)
9. Close in prayer. (1 min.)

Review Question: What are the five steps that can help determine God's leading? (See the boldface subheadings on pages 53–61 of the textbook.)

Discussion Questions: These do not necessarily have one right answer.

1. The authors talk about how they were gradually led into this ministry and constantly had to reevaluate their lives and resources. Discuss with the class if the church has gained an increased awareness of the need for such a ministry and if class members have made a conscious effort to show hospitality.

2. React to this statement: If your guest has to sleep on the floor, you never should have invited him. Discuss under what circumstances this might or might not be true.

3. Read I Kings 17:8–16. Discuss the faith that meets needs despite limited physical circumstances.

Thought Question: If you were aware of an urgent need for a homeless child, how could you creatively rearrange space to accommodate that child in your home?

Additional or Alternate Learning Activities

1. Ask those who have families to discuss with their children the possibility of bringing someone new into their households. Refer to a specific case such as a foster child, foreign student, etc. Also, list the different types of hospitality they and their families would be willing to practice. Have them give the summaries of their family discussions in class. Exchange views and ideas. Talk about overcoming practical obstacles (through the disciplined use of time and resources), as well as accepting that some types of hospitality are a "closed door." Once again apply the steps of God's leading to this discussion.

2. Work individually, as married couples, or in small groups on activity 3, page 61, sharing attributes of God and scriptural promises to calm your fears.

SESSION 7

The Recipient

I Corinthians 2:12–16

Teaching Objective: The student will be able to list three criteria for accepting the "alien and the stranger" into one's home. (See pages 67–70 of the textbook.)

Recommended Student Preparation

1. Read chapter 7 of the textbook.
2. Complete activities 1 and 4 before class.
3. Read I Corinthians 2:12–16.
4. If you want to use the alternate or additional activity, have a student prepare a report on chapter 16 of Vivian Hall's *Be My Guest.*

Recommended Leader Preparation

1. Be prepared to discuss from Vivian Hall's book what exceptions Scripture makes to opening one's household. See II Thessalonians 3:6–10; I Corinthians 5:9–11; and II John 7–11.
2. You may want to refer to the following books in the bibliography: Foster, 1978 and Hall, 1979, pages 84–88.
3. For the role-play of Steve Smith, ("Recommended Use of Class Time," number 6) you should round out his identity with specific rules that he has broken and more information about his home and community. Make it relevant to your church and community.

Recommended Use of Class Time: This assumes a 50-minute period.

1. Scripture reading: I Corinthians 2:12–16. Comment briefly: The spiritual man appraises all things because he has the mind of Christ. (3 min.)
2. Prayer. (2 min.)
3. Administrative matters. Attendance, etc. as required by your school. (2 min.)
4. Review the last two sessions by using some of their review questions. (5 min.)
5. Review the basic ideas in chapter 7 of the textbook. Then with the class, list on the overhead projector steps for establishing living terms and goals. (8 min.)
6. Use this teaching to lead into activity 3, page 72. Create a role-play with one student assuming the identity of Steve Smith. Two other members of the class should then play the role of the family making the decision. Try not to interrupt during the role-play with coaching, but do have a class member note the steps taken and record them on the overhead, which should be behind the backs of the "family." When the role-play is over, have the class discuss and critique it. Be sure to clear up through discussion any questions the class may have. (role-play—5 min.; critique—10 min.)
7. Divide the class into groups of three or four to review activities 1 and 4, which class members were to prepare. This involves looking at the group's own local situation to assess current needs and facilities. Each group should compile a list of both and hand them to the group leader. These will be used at the final class session. (13 min.)
8. Use review and discussion questions as time permits.
9. Give the assignment for next session. See recommended student preparation under the next session. (1 min.)
10. Close in prayer. (1 min.)

Review Question: State three main guidelines to use in determining if a person should be the recipient of radical hospitality. (See page 67.)

Discussion Questions: These do not necessarily have one right answer.

1. Have the class empathize with Steve Smith (class role-play). How might they feel if they were in his position, and how might they make the interview more comfortable for him?

2. Evaluate your ability to listen creatively with an open mind. Can you hear the difference between objective statements and emotionally charged story telling?

3. How does the use of Matthew 18:15–17 create the best conditions for fact finding and confrontations? How would applying these principles help you evaluate the newcomer's background, as well as future interaction?

Thought Question: Are you making it known to others in your church and community that you are available and eager to meet needs?

Additional or Alternate Learning Activities

1. Have the student give a book report from Vivian Hall's *Be My Guest.* Focus on chapter 16. Discuss briefly times when hospitality should be denied to a person. Have the class focus on refusal to repent and unwillingness to change lifestyles. (5 min.)

2. Do activity 2, page 71.

SESSION 8

Dealing with Parents

Ephesians 6:1–4; II Corinthians 5:17–21

Teaching Objective: The student will be able to list at least three ways to encourage constructive communication between natural parents and the extended family who are ministering to young people. (See the answer to review question 1.)

Recommended Student Preparation

1. Read the textbook, chapter 8.
2. Read Ephesians 6:1–4 and II Corinthians 5:17–21.
3. Complete activity 2 on page 84 of the textbook.

Recommended Leader Preparation

1. Ask a ministering family member (from outside your local church if necessary) to give a talk to the class about their dealing with rebellious teens and their parents. Prepare them by letting them know what you have been studying and by providing them with a copy of *Radical Hospitality* if they are not familiar with the book.

2. Scan the bibliography. You may want to give a brief summary of a chapter from *Teenage Rebellion* by Truman Dollar and Grace Ketterman.

Recommended Use of Class Time: This assumes a 50-minute period.

1. Scripture reading: Ephesians 6:1–4 and II Corinthians 5:17–21. (2 min.)

2. Prayer. (2 min.)

3. Administrative matters. Attendance, etc. as required by your school. (2 min.)

4. Have the guest speaker give his presentation about taking rebellious or problem teens into his home. Have the speaker discuss the blessings as well as the trials. Ask him to focus on the child's natural family's reactions. (10 min.)

5. Have the class ask questions. (5 min.)

6. On the overhead or marker board, list the major subheadings in this chapter:

   a. Seeing the Parent's Perspective
   b. Building Relationships
   c. Establishing Bounds
   d. Counseling for Parents
   e. Problems Parents Create

Solicit a twenty-five words or less summary of each division. (13 min.)

7. As a group, discuss the biblical principles in the Berachah Farm Family Resolve form (activity 2 on page 84) and work through the questions in that activity. (14 min.)

8. Use review and discussion questions as time permits.

9. Give the assignment for next session. See recommended student preparation under the next session. (1 min.)

10. Close in prayer. (1 min.)

Review Questions

1. List ways that encourage constructive communication between natural parents and the extended family. (Seeing the parent's perspective, keeping continuous communication, counseling parents, reminding the parents that they have more to lose if you fail, encouraging parents to build a bridge of communication with their child, and having a loving attitude.)

2. Give two examples of problems parents create. (Allowing jealousy of the foster parents to prevent progress, and fault finding, which may impede progress.)

3. What is one means of coming to see the parent's perspective? (See the textbook, page 75: listening!)

Discussion Questions: These do not necessarily have one right answer.

1. A young boy, John, has spent one month in your household learning to cooperate and accept authority. He has just returned from the first weekend visit with his natural family. John now is as angry and uncooperative as he was when he first came. What steps might you take to regain control?

2. Act out a disagreement between parent and child. Ask the class to be peacemakers. Have them spot the main problem and the complications caused by their unloving responses.

3. Why might you want to have your first interview with the child alone? What effect may the presence of the parents have on the child's answers?

4. Try to think of a time when you were a peacemaker in your family. How did you bring two warring people into peaceful acceptance of one another? How does one's attitude and spirit help or hinder a situation.

Additional or Alternate Learning Activities

1. Try role-playing discussion question number 1.
2. Use activity 2 on page 84 of the textbook.

SESSION 9

Setting Goals and Bounds, I

Philippians 3:13b, 14; Colossians 3:8–17

Teaching Objectives

1. The student will be able to explain why goals and bounds are necessary. (They are the best defense against manipulation.)

2. The student will be able to list the four main pieces of advice for radical hospitality given in this chapter. (1. Beware of manipulation. 2. Establish terms and bounds. 3. Have family meetings. 4. Learn from failure.)

Recommended Student Preparation

1. Read the textbook, chapter 9.
2. Read Philippians 3:13b, 14 and Colossians 3:8–17.

Recommended Leader Preparation

1. This is an extremely important chapter. We will spend two sessions on it.

2. Before class, prepare an overhead transparency with Philippians 3:13b, 14 on it.

Recommended Use of Class Time: This assumes a 50-minute period.

1. Prayer. (2 min.)

2. Administrative matters. Attendance, etc. as required by your school. (2 min.)

3. Review the last session by using some of its review questions. (5 min.)

4. Put the prepared overhead transparency of Philippians 3:13b, 14 on the overhead and ask why the verse is applicable to both host and guest in the hard day-to-day work of radical hospitality. (5 min.)

5. Study together Colossians 3:8–17, making a list of the putting off and the putting on that it teaches. (We will try to deal with two lists at the same time in this class. If necessary, put one on the marker board and one on the overhead.)

Put off: anger, wrath, malice, slander, abusive speech, and lying.

Put on: a heart of compassion, kindness, humility, gentleness, patience, forbearance, forgiveness, love, and peace. Briefly discuss each. Ask for an example of how each of the put on's is exercised. (10 min.)

6. Give the class five minutes to scan the chapter and outline the main points in their minds. Ask the class to give you the main headings and subheadings. List these on an overhead or marker board as they are given. A typical outline should look like the one below: (14 min.)

I. Beware of manipulation

II. Establish terms and bounds.

- A. Terms
  1. Need for work or study
  2. Care of the physical body
  3. Attendance at local church worship
- B. Bounds
  1. Use of family possessions
  2. Kitchen privileges
  3. Use of telephone
  4. Use of alcohol, drugs, and tobacco
  5. Private space

III. Family meetings

IV. Learning from failure

---

7. From the chapter outline, look again at your list of put off's and put on's. How do they relate? (10 min.)

8. Use review and discussion questions as time permits.

9. Give the assignment for next session. See recommended student preparation under the next session. (1 min.)

10. Close in prayer. (1 min.)

Review Questions

1. What are four pieces of advice the authors give to those who are exercising radical hospitality? (1. Beware of manipulation. 2. Establish terms and bounds. 3. Have family meetings. 4. Learn from failure.)

2. List matters that need to be considered in establishing terms for a recipient of radical hospitality. (See the chapter outline above.)

3. List matters that need to be considered in establishing bounds for a recipient of radical hospitality. (See the chapter outline above.)

4. List some of the things Colossians 3:8–17 tells us to put off.

5. List some of the things Colossians 3:8–17 tells us to put on.

Discussion Questions: These do not necessarily have one right answer.

1. How does labeling a person "student" in his learning role help in his growth and cooperation with those labeled "teachers"?

2. Other than the reasons already mentioned, discuss why an interview with a prospective guest should include a review of *written* house rules. (Look for an answer that relates to written rules as a precaution against a host's *understating* his carefully developed rules when, during an interview, he is trying to make his nervous guest feel at ease.)

3. Why might we feel uncomfortable presenting a list of bounds to our new family member? Would you be able to explain why you have such rules?

SESSION **10**

Setting Goals and Bounds, II

I Corinthians 3:6–11

Teaching Objective: The student will be able to write a list of possible bounds that fit his particular living situation.

Recommended Student Preparation

1. Read the textbook, chapter 9.
2. Do the activities on page 101.
3. Write a set of bounds that apply to your household. (Activity 3, page 101.)

Recommended Leader Preparation

1. Ask a ministering family member who has dealt with unemployed or maladjusted adults to speak to the class. Remember to explain to him what you have been studying and provide him with a copy of *Radical Hospitality* if he is unfamiliar with it.
2. Look at Adams's *Godliness Through Discipline* and Augsberger's *Caring Enough to Confront.*

Recommended Use of Class Time: This assumes a 50-minute period.

1. Scripture reading: I Corinthians 3:6–11. (2 min.)
2. Prayer. (2 min.)
3. Administrative matters. Attendance, etc. as required by your school. (2 min.)
4. Have the guest speaker give his presentation about

ministering to maladjusted adults. Ask questions pertaining to setting bounds. (talk—10 min.; questions—5 min.)

5. Review the previous session by using its review questions. (5 min.)

6. Review activities 1, 2, and 4 briefly. (10 min.)

7. Review the assignment to write a set of bounds for the students' homes: Ask the class members to share some of the bounds they have established. Then present the following hypothetical situations. Do the bounds help or apply in these situations? Did you leave out some bounds you should have included? (12 min.)

a. A pregnant, unmarried, young woman enters your home. She will be placing her baby for adoption. She is quiet, very shy, and very unsure of herself. (Response?)

1) After she has spent several weeks in your home, you return from an evening out to find an intoxicated, loud, young man in your living room. You ask him to leave and he does. (Response?)

2) Two weeks later, your guest asks if she can have the young man visit again. He is the father of her child. (Response?)

b. A brash young man in his late twenties has had his wife walk out on him. He needs a place to rethink matters and change. He is one of those know-it-all types. (Response?)

1) The young man's car is in the garage and he asks to borrow yours for about an hour to do some shopping. (Response?)

2) You get a call two hours later. The young man has been in an accident. There was a serious injury in the other vehicle. The young man did not have a driver's license. (Response?)

8. Use review and discussion questions as time permits.

9. Give the assignment for the next session. See recommended student preparation under the next session. (1 min.)

10. Close in prayer. (1 min.)

Review Questions: The questions from the last session apply to this session also.

Discussion Questions: These do not necessarily have one right answer.

1. How would ministering to foreign students or other cross-cultural situations affect your household? How could you bridge the gap between differences in environment and thought?

2. If a new family member is required to take part in family devotions, how might you find creative ways to keep him interested?

SESSION 11

The Local Church

Ephesians 4:11–16; I Corinthians 12:18–20

Teaching Objective: The student will be able to define the role of the local church in the ministry of radical hospitality as providing support in terms of prayer, physical relief, and supplementary resources.

Recommended Student Preparation

1. Read the textbook, chapter 10.
2. Read Ephesians 4:11–16 and I Corinthians 12:18–20.
3. Complete activities 1 and 2 on page 108.

Recommended Leader Preparation

1. Acquire the words and music to "Blest Be the Tie."
2. Scan *The Equipping Ministry* by Paul Benjamin. You may want to look at certain parts in more depth. You may want a student to give a book report on it.

Recommended Use of Class Time: This assumes a 50-minute period.

1. Scripture reading: Ephesians 4:11–16. (2 min.)
2. Prayer. (2 min.)
3. Administrative matters. Attendance, etc. as required by your school. (2 min.)
4. Begin by asking the class members to sing together the hymn "Blest Be the Tie," especially noting the second and third verses. Then read together I Corinthians 12:18–20 as a beginning focus. (4 min.)

5. Review the authors' model for radical hospitality and explain that today's session will discuss in detail the role of the local church. Study together Ephesians 4:11–16 as a reminder of the body concept, which Scripture emphasizes. (10 min.)

6. List the three subheadings of chapter 10 of the textbook on an overhead or marker board. Ask for a twenty-five words or less explanation of what the authors said under each heading. (14 min.)

7. Divide into groups of three or four to compile a list of resources available among the local church people. Also have each group member share his responses to the activities given as an assignment for this session. These lists should be given to the class leader for use in the final session. (12 min.)

8. Use review and discussion questions as time permits.

9. Give the assignment for next session. See recommended student preparation under the next session. (1 min.)

10. Close by singing "Blest Be the Tie," this time as a commitment to support each other. (3 min.)

Review Questions

1. What three ways can the local church support you in exercising radical hospitality? (Prayer, physical relief, and supplementary resources—textbook, bottom of page 103 and top of 104.)

2. What role does the local church leadership (the board of elders in presbyterian churches) have to play in your exercising radical hospitality. (They can give advice on difficult decisions—textbook, page 104.)

3. What sort of resources besides those usually called spiritual can a local church provide. (Many members possess skills that can be helpful in providing the newcomer with new habits and productivity—textbook, page 107.)

Discussion Questions: These do not necessarily have one right answer.

1. Would knowing that someone is willing to give you an occasional weekend off from your ministry make it easier to have a long-term commitment to radical hospitality?

2. What are the many benefits the new family member will experience as he becomes part of the lives of many church families?

3. What are dangers church members will have to guard against as they have contact with both the host family and the new family member? What does James 3:2–18 say about the tongue and its use for healing and destruction? Apply this to the temptations to unwisely confide unedifying facts as we live and interact with each.

4. How might the zeal to convince others of the necessity of radical hospitality work counter to the conviction of the Holy Spirit?

Additional or Alternate Activity: Ask a student to do a book report on *The Equipping Ministry* by Paul Benjamin.

SESSION 12

Prayer

Philippians 1:9–11

Teaching Objectives

1. The student will be able to state at least three occasions when prayer is needed in radical hospitality.

2. The student will be able to give at least three passages of Scripture that instruct us how to pray.

Recommended Student Preparation

1. Read chapter 11 of the textbook.

2. Read Philippians 1:9–11. Note the elements in Paul's prayer in the Philippian passage that would apply to radical hospitality, and be prepared to show how each applies.

Recommended Use of Class Time: This assumes a 50-minute period.

1. Scripture reading: Philippians 1:9–11. (2 min.)

2. Prayer. (2 min.)

3. Administrative matters. Attendance, etc. as required by your school. (2 min.)

4. Review the previous sessions by using the following questions: What are the three components of radical hospitality? (A ministering family, a local church, and a recipient.) What is the contribution of each? If you have all three elements, is an effective ministry insured? Why not? (5 min.)

5. Have various students read the following passages of

Scripture and relate what they teach about how one should pray in each situation. After each student has answered, allow the class to interact.

a. When angry: Psalm 4

b. When needing protection: II Thessalonians 3:1–5 and Romans 15:30–32

c. When needing love: Ephesians 3:14–21

d. When desiring to see the gospel spread: Colossians 4:2–4. (12 min.)

6. Discuss together the authors' concern for praying without ceasing, and when in radical hospitality one should focus on personal prayer, when on corporate and family prayer, and when on prayer with the new family member. (8 min.)

7. Before spending time in group prayer, share with each other the homework assignment. (8 min.)

8. Close in prayer: Pray together for the group's venture into radical hospitality, using Paul's teachings on prayer and adding the particulars of the group's situation. Pray too for those whom the group may know who are currently in this ministry. (10 min.)

9. Give the assignment for the next session. See recommended student preparation under the next session. (1 min.)

10. Use the review and discussion questions only if time permits.

Review Question: What are four things those engaged in radical hospitality should pray for? (See the subheadings in chapter 11 of the textbook.)

Discussion Question: This does not necessarily have one right answer. Discuss the concept of quietly waiting on the Lord? What does this mean. Explore the anatomy of a quietness and peace that sheds all distractions and clears the mind for God to speak through His Word. (You may want to refer to Karen Main's book, pages 192-93.)

Additional or Alternate Learning Activity: You may want to do the activities on page 118 of the textbook.

SESSION **13**

Building the Local Model

I Corinthians 1:4–9

Teaching Objective: The student will be able to state at least three basic concepts relating to radical hospitality that have been learned during the course.

Recommended Student Preparation

1. Read I Corinthians 1:4–9.
2. Spend some time in prayer regarding the role you should play in the local church's radical hospitality ministry.

Recommended Leader Preparation: Three things should be covered in this last session:

1. Review: Go over the whole course to make sure everyone has a grasp of the basic points.
2. Evaluation: Were the goals and objectives accomplished? What could have been handled better? How can you improve your teaching? How can we improve our guide?
3. Application: If the class has been moved to exercise radical hospitality, now is the time to act. What can be done?

For one of the activities you will need in hand the lists compiled in sessions 7 and 11.

Recommended Use of Class Time: This assumes a 50-minute period.

1. Prayer. (2 min.)
2. Administrative matters. Attendance, etc. as required by

your school. (2 min.)

3. Review: Use review questions from various sessions. Look also at the objectives. Are the students able to . . .? It is best not to use the discussion questions when reviewing. (10 min.)

4. Evaluate: The course, the materials, and the teacher. (11 min.)

5. Act: What can we now do? (11 min.)

a. Read I Corinthians 1:4–9 and discuss the encouragement found there. Emphasize that God has given His grace and has provided that no spiritual gift is lacking.

b. Solicit sharing from the students. Do any feel there are indications of God's leading them to act in radical hospitality?

c. Using the lists compiled in sessions 7 and 11, make definite plans to help anyone who has decided to open his home to the stranger and alien. If no one has so decided, resolve to continue to study the need and make contingency plans to meet needs that might arise.

6. Close with a prayer time for the ministry of radical hospitality in your area. Ask the class members to share any specific requests. (14 min.)

BIBLIOGRAPHY

Adams, Jay. *Christian Living in the Home.* Phillipsburg, NJ: Presbyterian and Reformed, 1972. Adams establishes that the family is composed of sinners, but sinners in the process of change as they love, forgive, and work through their rough spots together.

__________ . *Godliness Through Discipline.* Phillipsburg, NJ: Presbyterian and Reformed, 1972. A short but helpful booklet that will aid the new family member to grow in the discipline needed to change his habits and life.

Augsberger, David. *Caring Enough to Confront.* Glendale, CA: Regal, 1973. Augsberger's goal is to develop the reader's skills in objective, clear confrontation.

Benjamin, Paul. *The Equipping Ministry.* Cincinnati: Standard Press, 1978. A tool for church leaders to assist church families in finding and exercising spiritual gifts.

Bonhoeffer, Dietrich. *Life Together.* New York: Harper and Row, 1952. A classic treatment of the church as a community.

Bubeck, Mark. *The Adversary.* Chicago: Moody Press, 1979. This book is filled with prayer examples that are helpful in praying against the world, the flesh, and the devil, making prayer offensive rather than defensive.

DeVaux, Roland. *Ancient Israel, Vol. 1.* New York: McGraw Hill, 1965. A scholarly work that deals with the biblical practices of ancient Israel related to the alien and the stranger in the land.

Dollar, Truman and Ketterman, Grace. *Teenage Rebellion.* Old Tappan, NJ: Fleming H. Revell, 1979. This book will help most parents who have rebellious children analyze reasons for their child's behavior. It will give the ministering family a basis for tackling the problems the guest child brings into the home.

Enroth, Ronald. *The Lure of the Cults.* Chappaqua, NY: Christian Herald Books, 1979. Enroth gives insight into the psychological and sociological pulls and trends of society that draw youth into cults. The need for a sense of purpose and for a family can be met for many through radical hospitality.

Foster, Richard J. *The Celebration of Discipline.* New York: Harper and Row, 1978. A very helpful book on all areas of spiritual discipline. The chapters on prayer meditation, and corporate guidance are most applicable here.

__________ . *The Freedom of Simplicity.* New York: Harper and Row, 1981. This book gives many insights into Old Testament practices, such as the year of the jubilee, that were designed to keep the people of God from materialism and to break the cycle of the poor and needy in Israel.

Hall, Vivian Anderson. *Be My Guest.* Chicago: Moody Press, 1979. This book deals with the various methods of hospitality and gives practical tips for carrying them out. She also gives necessary attention to the type of person to whom we should not show hospitality.

Jackson, David and Neta. *Living Together in a World Coming Apart.* Carol Stream, IL: Creation House, 1974. While the

Jacksons make their case for Christian community over against an individualized lifestyle, they do offer an excellent exposure to the benefits and blessings of extended households.

Mack, Wayne A. *A Homework Manual for Biblical Counseling, Vol. I.* Phillipsburg, NJ: Presbyterian and Reformed, 1981. This book is excellent reference material for finding particular Scripture to deal with particular sins.

__________. *Strengthening Your Marriage* (formerly *How to Develop Deep Unity in the Marriage Relationship).* Phillipsburg, NJ: Presbyterian and Reformed, 1977. This is an indispensable guide for a married couple to evaluate their commitment to the Lord and each other before considering radical hospitality.

Mains, Karen. *The Key to a Loving Heart.* Elgin, IL: David C. Cook, 1979. Much is taught about forgiveness, that key to a loving heart, which is an essential quality for radical hospitality.

__________. *Open Heart, Open Home.* Elgin, IL: David C. Cook, 1975. Mains establishes the biblical foundation for hospitality, leading to a proper view of stewardship of time and possessions in using the home for the Lord. A basic foundational book for any hospitality ministry.

Milliken, Bill. *Tough Love.* Old Tappan, NJ: Fleming H. Revell, 1968. The story of a New York City youth worker who realized he had to set limits and bounds in order for people to change.

O'Brien, Bev. *"Mom, I'm Pregnant."* Wheaton, IL: Tyndale, 1982. To the pregnant, out of wedlock, young woman, radical hospitality can offer healing and forgiveness. The author gives effective counsel on this issue, which often alienates children from their parents.

Perkins, John. *A Quiet Revolution.* Waco, TX: Word Books, 1977. An excellent book exposing the failure of the evangelical church to meet the needs of the poor in our society. Perkins expressively describes how the poor are "locked in," but continues by offering strategy and solutions for the church.

Rinker, Rosalind. *How to Have Family Prayer.* Grand Rapids: Zondervan, 1979. This well-known author on the subject of prayer offers suggestions on overcoming the fear of praying aloud and overcoming the obstacles that keep family devotions from being successful.

Schaeffer, Edith. *L'Abri.* Wheaton, IL: Tyndale House, 1969. The story of the establishment of this well-known Christian community with helpful and inspiring ideas for the local church.

__________ . *What Is a Family?* Old Tappan, NJ: Fleming H. Revell, 1975. Schaeffer not only assesses the spiritual condition of the nuclear family, but also gives advice on keeping this biologically related entity strong while providing a substitute family for others.

Snyder, Howard A. *The Community of the King.* Downers Grove, IL: InterVarsity Press, 1977. Snyder shows the importance of the church as a caring community, the basic truth that must be understood in radical hospitality.

Toffler, Alvin. *The Third Wave.* New York: Bantam, 1981. While this is not a Christian book, Toffler projects a growing psychological and sociological need for "life-organizing" groups and households to help people burned out and disillusioned by a high-tech society.